Zac Efron

Katie Franks

PowerKiDS press
New York

To JC, the keeper of the flame

Published in 2009 by The Rosen Publishing Group, Inc.
29 East 21st Street, New York, NY 10010

First Edition

Editor: Nicole Pristash
Book Design: Kate Laczynski
Photo Researcher: Jessica Gerweck

Photo Credits: Cover, pp. 4, 7, 11, 15, 16, 20 © Getty Images; p. 12 © Jemal Countess/Getty Images; p. 8 © Jeff Vespa/Getty Images; p. 19 © David James/Zuma Press; p. 20 © Vera Anderson/Getty Images.

Library of Congress Cataloging-in-Publication Data

Franks, Katie.
  Zac Efron / Katie Franks. — 1st ed.
      p. cm. — (Kid stars!)
  Includes index.
  ISBN 978-1-4042-4465-8 (library binding) ISBN 978-1-4042-4530-3 (pbk)
  ISBN 978-1-4042-4548-8 (6-pack)
  1. Efron, Zac—Juvenile literature. 2. Actors—United States—Biography—Juvenile literature. I. Title.
  PN2287.E395F73 2009
  792.02'8092—dc22
  [B]
                                        2007050676

Manufactured in the United States of America

Contents

Zac Efron is one of the biggest teen stars in America. His fans cannot wait to see what he does next.

Meet Zac Efron

Zac Efron has become a huge star ever since he appeared in the Disney Channel's 2006 movie *High School Musical*. This talented young man not only acts, but he also sings and dances. **Millions** of fans around the world are drawn to his talent and good looks.

To get where he is today, Zac has had to work very hard since childhood. He stands ready to make the tricky move from kid star to adult star. Let's get a peek at Zac's rise to fame and what we may expect from him next!

Zac's Childhood

Zachary David Alexander Efron was born on October 18, 1987. His mother and father are Starla and David Efron, and his younger brother is named Dylan. Zac's family is of Jewish **ancestry**, but Zac does not practice any **religion**.

Zac grew up in Arroyo Grande, California, which is between San Francisco and Los Angeles. Growing up, Zac was a good student. He worked hard to get straight As, and he often got mad if he got a B. Zac liked to have fun, though. He was known as the class clown because the other kids thought he was so funny!

Here Zac is seen shooting a basketball with his fans. Zac played basketball in sixth grade, but he says he was the worst player on his team!

Zac has a strong singing voice. He even practices at home.
Zac says the first thing he does in the morning is sing!

A Young Actor

Zac started acting when he was 11 years old. In 1998, he tried out for a role, or part, in the musical *Gypsy* at his town's **theater**. Zac quickly fell in love with acting and being onstage. Zac enjoyed it so much that he decided to take singing and acting **lessons** so he could get even better.

After taking lessons for a while, Zac and his family thought Zac should try his luck at being a **professional** actor. This meant going to Los Angeles where a lot of acting jobs are.

Getting TV Work

In 2002, when he was 15, Zac and his mother drove to Los Angeles three days a week to **audition** for acting parts. Auditioning was hard. Zac was turned down a lot. Zac said that for every role he won, he was turned down for at least 30 others! He kept trying, though.

Zac soon landed small roles on TV shows. In 2004, he got the role of Cameron Bale on the WB show *Summerland*. It ended in 2005, but Zac's role got him noticed. It led to his biggest role yet, his role in *High School Musical*.

Being an actor is hard work. Zac believes you really have to love acting to handle getting turned down at auditions.

Zac (second from right) and the other stars of
High School Musical are close friends. Here they are seen at
The Today Show in 2006.

High School Musical

In *High School Musical*, Zac plays Troy, a basketball player. One New Year's Eve, Troy discovers his love of music while singing **karaoke** with Gabriella, played by Vanessa Hudgens. Even though Troy and Gabriella are very different from each other, they audition for their high school's musical. Many people try to stop them, but Troy and Gabriella show the other students how to like one another for who they are.

High School Musical was a surprise hit. More than 26 million people watched it its first week on TV. *High School Musical* made Zac and the other cast members instant stars.

More Musicals

    Since *High School Musical* was so **popular**, Disney decided to make a **sequel**. *High School Musical 2* came out in 2007. In the movie, Troy and his friends have a talent show at the country club where many of the kids have summer jobs. *High School Musical 2* was a big hit. Most fans loved it just as much as the first movie.

    Because of this, Zac had to quickly learn how to deal with his fame. He does not let it change him, though. Zac has said that even though he is famous, he is still the same person.

Zac enjoys having fans, but he does not always understand why they like him so much. He says he is very boring in real life!

15

Singing is a big part of Zac's life. Zac was happy that *High School Musical 2* gave his fans the chance to hear him sing well.

Zac Sings!

Many fans love the **sound tracks** for the *High School Musical* movies. Fans sing and dance to the songs just like the actors in the movies do. Some of the songs have even been Top 40 hits!

Zac was not happy with the sound track for the first movie, though. Troy's songs were written for a singer with a higher voice than Zac's. Zac's voice was then mixed with another singer's voice. To prove that he could sing well, Zac pushed for the chance to sing in the sequel. In *High School Musical 2*, Zac sings by himself.

Hairspray

In 2006, when he was 18, Zac landed a role in the movie *Hairspray*, which is based on the Broadway musical *Hairspray*. Zac played Link Larkin, a boy on a TV dance show in his hometown. Like in *High School Musical 2*, Zac got to do his own singing.

Zac was proud of his work in the movie. He got to work with famous actors, such as John Travolta and Amanda Bynes. By taking such a big role, Zac was able to show off his talents to audiences who may not have seen the *High School Musical* movies. Many people loved *Hairspray* and it was a big hit for Zac.

Hairspray takes place in 1962. To help Zac play his character, Zac's mother told him what boys were like during that time.

When picking the movies he will work on next, Zac often thinks about his fans. He picks characters and movies that will take his fans along on a fun ride!

What's Next?

Zac has a bright road ahead of him. After the third *High School Musical* movie, he will be seen in the movie *Seventeen*. In this movie, Zac plays an adult who is turned back into a 17-year-old.

Unlike his *High School Musical* cast mates, Zac has not put out a music album. He wants to work on his acting instead and sing only if the role calls for it. Zac has big dreams for acting, though. He hopes to start playing more adult roles. Zac also hopes to one day play an action hero! Fans will surely see Zac in many different types of roles, big and small.

ZAC EFRON

 Zac is 5 feet 9 inches (1.75 m) tall.

 Zac is learning to play the guitar.

 Zac loves sports. He likes skiing, rock climbing, and snowboarding.

 Zac and his family love animals. They have two dogs, Dreamer and Puppy, and a cat, Simon.

 He is a big fan of the San Francisco Giants baseball team.

 The *High School Musical* star graduated from, or finished, Arroyo Grande High School in 2006.

 One of Zac's most valued **collections** is his collection of signed baseballs.

 Zac likes the cartoon *Rocko's Modern Life*.

 Zac likes to work on cars. He has a 1965 Mustang that he got from his grandfather.

 Zac wishes he could be a superhero.

Glossary

ancestry (AN-ses-tree) Having to do with a person's relatives who lived long ago.

audition (ah-DIH-shun) To test the skills of an actor.

collections (kuh-LEK-shunz) Groups of objects that are alike and saved over time.

karaoke (ker-ee-OH-kee) An activity during which people sing the words to songs while a machine plays the music.

lessons (LEH-sunz) Things that you learn from or study.

millions (MIL-yunz) Very large numbers.

musical (MYOO-zih-kul) A play or movie that has singing and dancing.

popular (PAH-pyuh-lur) Liked by lots of people.

professional (pruh-FESH-nul) Someone who is paid for what he does.

religion (rih-LIH-jen) A belief in and a way of honoring a god or gods.

sequel (SEE-kwel) A movie with the same characters and setting as an earlier movie.

sound tracks (SOWND TRAX) Music albums that go with a movie or TV show.

theater (THEE-uh-tur) A building where plays and movies are shown.

Index

Web Sites

Due to the changing nature of Internet links, PowerKids Press has developed an online list of Web sites related to the subject of this book. This site is updated regularly. Please use this link to access the list:
www.powerkidslinks.com/kids/zefron/